GOODNIGHT, GRACIE

Phoenix Poets

A SERIES EDITED BY ROBERT VON HALLBERG

LLOYD SCHWARTZ

Goodnight, Gracie

THE UNIVERSITY OF CHICAGO PRESS
Chicago and London

Lloyd Schwartz, co-director of the Creative Writing Program at the University of Massachusetts-Boston, is the classical music editor of The Boston Phoenix *and a regular commentator on National Public Radio's* Fresh Air.

The University of Chicago Press, Chicago 60637
The University of Chicago Press, Ltd., London
© 1992 by The University of Chicago
All rights reserved. Published 1992
Printed in the United States of America

00 99 98 97 96 95 94 93 92   5 4 3 2 1

ISBN (cloth): 0-226-74204-0
ISBN (paper): 0-226-74205-9

Library of Congress Cataloging-in-Publication Data

Schwartz, Lloyd, 1941-
     Goodnight, Gracie / Lloyd Schwartz.
       p. cm.—(Phoenix poets)
     I. Title.   II. Series.
   PS3569.C5667G66   1992
   811'.54—dc20   *91-25826*
                                                            CIP

⊚ *The paper used in this publication meets the minimum requirements of the American National Standard for Information Sciences—Permanence of Paper for Printed Library Materials, ANSI Z39.48-1984.*

For my mother, Ida Singer Schwartz

Contents

Acknowledgments

The author would like to express special gratitude to the National Endowment for the Arts, the Somerville Arts Council, and the Pushcart Press, as well as to the editors of *The Best American Poetry 1991* and to the editors and publishers of the following magazines, in which these poems first appeared.

Agni: "Crossing the Rockies"
Grand Street: "Dead-Battery Blues," "Goodnight, Gracie," "House Hunting," "In the Jewish Cemetery in Queens"
The Massachusetts Review: "Vermeers," © 1987 The Massachusetts Review, Inc.
The New Republic: "Leaves"
Pequod: "Gisela Brüning"
Ploughshares: "Accomplice," "In the Mist," "Pseudodoxia Epidemica," "Reports of My Death"
Poetry: "Love"
Shenandoah: "Fourteen People," "Simple Questions"

one

Reports of My Death

1. Heroic Measures

My friend deals with each new wrinkle in his illness as if it weren't one more step toward the inevitable catastrophe.

Always a loner (he claims), he's now tasting the sweetnesses of friendship for the first time. His thirty-year writing block dissolved: grim, heartbreaking poems—pulled, he says, from the "iron jaws" of his disease. He recites the last one aloud to himself, to cheer himself up.

He argues with his wife. She wants him to keep up his strength, but he has no appetite.

> "It's the antibiotics," she tells him.
> "It's the cancer," he says.

He's been talking to his doctor about "last things." He rejects "heroic measures" merely to be kept alive. He doesn't want to die in pain.

> "Is the pain worse?" she asks.
> "It's worse," he says.

"A lot worse?"

"Pain is evil," he says.

In the hospital, family and friends gather every day. When he can't speak, he writes nearly indecipherable notes on a large yellow pad. "I love you both," he scrawls with effort to two of us, "in the same breath." Soon he's too tired to write.

Then he can't write.

2. A Scare (1969)

A lump the size of a small walnut appears suddenly under my collarbone. Alarmed, my doctor rushes me into the hospital for "a minor exploratory procedure." The lump, he tells me afterwards, "was not evil."

The anaesthetic, I remember, makes me sick—so wobbly, a visiting friend's new husband has to help me into the bathroom.

The surgeon can't figure out what caused the lump. He asks me if I take heroin.

The scar near my collarbone continues to fade. When I go for checkups, my doctor still feels for the lump. Every year he asks: "Did that lump ever come back?"

I remember thinking: *"A few more days, it would've probably just gone away!"*

3. Reports of My Death

I'm at a concert, listening to Schubert's last quartet. The chilling quietude—celebration and mourning in every sumptuous, unearthly phrase.

He died at 31. Mozart was nearly 36; Keats only 25.

> *"That's the advantage of dying young—"* (Antonioni, *La Notte*), *"one escapes success."*

—This morning's phone call: "Is Lloyd OK? I heard he died!"

Died? I'm still shivering . . . Who started this rumor? My picture in the paper (I'd won an award) with a black box around it—had someone not read the caption?

Or could it have been deliberate? Some malicious joke?

"Isaac Bickerstaff, Esq." (aka Jonathan Swift)—first predicting, later *describing,* the death of Mr. John Partridge, detested astrologer.

Poor Partridge! After Swift's nasty prophecy "came true," friends rushed from him in horror, as if they'd seen a ghost.

> *"The reports of my death,"* Mark Twain remarked, *"are greatly exaggerated."*

Who'd wish me dead? Haven't I tried to be good—a good person, a good friend; "there" when needed; a good listener; forthright, but never deliberately cruel?

They'd say I was good at saying what was wanted to be heard—my "sympathy" self-serving, calculated not to give too much away.

They'd say I talked too much, took too much pleasure in gossip (and let nothing interfere with my pleasure). They'd say: "He made the phone company rich."

. . . A disgruntled student? Someone stung by one of my reviews?

"He had high standards. He demanded as much from others as he demanded of himself. He was unkind only when it was deserved."

But who deserves unkindness?

—And what monument did *he* build more lasting than bronze?

> *b. Brooklyn, 1941; d. Somerville, 1989. B.A.*
> *1962, Ph.D. 1976. English prof. Editor (see Bishop,*
> *Elizabeth). Mus. critic. Bk. of poems. No survivors.*

The hole I leave, shrinking like a silent-movie fade . . .

> *Poor POPE will grieve a Month; and GAY*
> *A Week; and ARBUTHNOT a Day.*
> *ST. JOHN himself will scarce forbear,*
> *To bite his Pen, and drop a Tear.*
>
> > (Jonathan Swift, "Verses on the Death of Dr. Swift")

In my car, I'm unusually cautious: the "fatal" truck about to shoot through the next intersection. Some kid rushes into the street—my foot slams on the brake; the driver behind me slams on his . . . The child, unconscious

of his brush with fate—unhit, unhurt—racing heedlessly home; he could have died in pain . . .

Did he look like me? (Did he *want* to die?)

My friends protest, try to reassure me, remind me that I'm still alive. But I still don't believe them.

> *"Lovely service. Good turnout."*
> *"So sudden! At least he didn't suffer long."*
> *"He worked too hard."*
> *"I thought he was a hypochondriac . . ."*

Is this what it feels like: the hollow coffin, the narrow plot, the lonely stone, the dates?

Mozart, Keats—

I died too soon. I hadn't finished perfecting myself.

Schubert—his last quartet racing heedlessly to its end. Is the concert over already?

Hart Crane, García Lorca, Emily Brontë, Felix Mendelssohn, Jane Austen, Sir Thomas Wyatt, Poe: I outlived you all—

How can I make my comeback from the grave?

L e a v e s

1

Every October it becomes important, no, *necessary*
to see the leaves turning, to be surrounded
by leaves turning; it's not just the symbolism,
to confront in the death of the year your death,
one blazing farewell appearance, though the irony
isn't lost on you that nature is most seductive
when it's about to die, flaunting the dazzle of its
incipient exit, an ending that at least so far
the effects of human progress (pollution, acid rain)
have not yet frightened you enough to make you believe
is real; that is, you know this ending is a deception
because of course nature is always renewing itself—
            the trees don't *die,* they just pretend,
            go out in style, and return in style: a new style.

2

Is it deliberate how far they make you go
especially if you live in the city to get far
enough away from home to see not just trees
but only trees? The boring highways, roadsigns, high

speeds, 10-axle trucks passing you as if they were
in an even greater hurry than you to look at leaves:
so you drive in terror for literal hours and it looks
like rain, or *snow,* but it's probably just clouds
(too cloudy to see any color?) and you wonder,
given the poverty of your memory, which road had the
most color last year, but it doesn't matter since
you're probably too late anyway, or too early—
>   whichever road you take will be the wrong one
>   and you've probably come all this way for nothing.

3

You'll be driving along depressed when suddenly
a cloud will move and the sun will muscle through
and ignite the hills. It may not last. Probably
won't last. But for a moment the whole world
comes to. Wakes up. Proves it lives. It lives—
red, yellow, orange, brown, russet, ocher, vermilion,
gold. Flame and rust. Flame and rust, the permutations
of burning. You're on fire. Your eyes are on fire.
It won't last, you don't want it to last. You
can't stand any more. But you don't want it to stop.
It's what you've come for. It's what you'll
come back for. It won't stay with you, but you'll
>   remember that it felt like nothing else you've felt
>   or something you've felt that also didn't last.

Gisela Brüning

Why should I remember now? More than 20 years . . . The Paris
Opéra! My first trip to Europe.

In the next box: Gisela Brüning and her handsome
blond son. Had she sensed how lonely I was—

or just how uncomfortable, craning
from the back of my box to see the stage?

". . . Maybe you would like to join us?"

They helped me over the partition (an usherette
       outside, on guard against people
       sneaking in where they didn't belong).

Her English was good; her son's
       better . . . He'd have been 16—small for his age,
       with a tense, serious look on his pale,
       baby face; I was 24 . . .
                     "From Hamburg, we are.
My husband stays at home."

(They resisted my attempt at German: I was
their opportunity to practice English.)

Even from the Brünings' front-row seats, the opera was
    hard to see. *Roméo et Juliette*—
                            singers I'd
    never heard of. The soprano, "mature" for
    Juliet, wore a hip-length blond wig.
    (At least she could sing the famous Waltz.)

Our discussions animated the intermissions. Past midnight,
    lingering near the Metro, we eventually
    decided to meet next day. Gisela
    wanted Holger to see Chartres—

    so we went to Chartres.

            .   .   .

They embarrassed me, and I was embarrassed
    for them, these cultivated travelers turned
    tourist stereotype—
                            shouting to each other from
    opposite ends of the vaulted nave: f-stops and
    light-meters; which film; what scene to shoot.

    (One photo they'd send—a chapel with
    burning candles—came out rather well.)

    "It is good to remember such scenes," Gisela said.

            .   .   .

We corresponded. Each air-letter had a motherly
    postscript: concerts they'd heard;
    museums she'd taken Holger to.

And the same invitation: Wouldn't I
        please visit? There was a bed for me. Plenty
        to eat. Operas. Museums. Hamburg was a
        great city: so very many fine things to do—

        please do not refuse.

                  . . .

The following summer, I planned a trip to Greece—and a week
        with the Brünings. (They'd have loved to come
        with me: Gisela wanted Holger to see Greece.)

                  . . .

Would I mind? Holger had written they were
        vegetarians. And sure enough:
                              sunflower seeds and
        raisins for breakfast; sunflower-seed-and-
        raisin sandwiches for lunch. Bowls of
        seeds and raisins on the table all day long.

        In the War, Gisela and her husband were forced to eat
        stray cats (if they were lucky to find any)—

        she could never eat meat again.

Herr Brüning was much older than his attractive,
        high-strung wife:
                              reticent, accommodating,
        avuncular (more Dutch than German?); happy to be
        so thoughtfully taken care of; "courtly."

And proud of his only son's accomplishments: first oboe
in his high school band (though too
shy to practice at home).

. . .

Gisela took us to the museum. She loved
the German expressionists—recognized
where all this luxury of color

could lead, but loved the danger
too, the brinksmanship.

Holger followed where she led, debating light-meters
and floor-plans (how to get "There" from "Here").

Gisela hardly minded contradiction from such a clever
boy who knew his own mind (even if she was never
completely convinced he was correct)—

they argued like sparrows.

. . .

We went to the opera. One night,
 Rigoletto: arias in Italian, choruses in German;

once, Benjamin Britten's *Ein Sommernachtstraum*—
a midsummer night's dream of a production (all lights
and shadows); its sublime quartet

of awakening lovers . . .

. . .

She took us to the red-light district. Young men, she said,
        should know about such things (and it was
        Hamburg's most famous attraction).

Olive-drab military barriers guarded each end of one
        narrow street:
                        rows of narrow houses
        with wide, open windows; buxom women leaning down
        and out in gaudy peasant blouses (low-cut
        elastic bodices digging into fleshy chests);

        crowds of men cruising, stopping to inspect, to
        "negotiate."

We nudged and giggled, but Gisela was serious. She
        approved of this system. Men, she said,
        need to be relieved of their tensions.
                                And at least
        these women were forced to stay clean.

Holger's outspoken, enlightened mother made him blush.

                · · ·

They took me to meet Holger's English teacher (his favorite).
        Distinguished, dapper, his suit meticulously
        pressed—he pressed my hand, pressed
        me to return . . .
                        But Gisela had every minute planned:

        so many interesting things for a visitor to do.

                · · ·

One excursion took us to Lübeck: Bach's church; Thomas Mann's
    house;
        bathing cabinets, bikinis, and naked
    children frolicking in the gray Baltic.

Was this the field trip I have the photo from? Holger in
    lederhosen, I in my brown English raincoat;
    a deserted grassy ridge.
                    We're perched on a bench,
    sitting on our crossed legs, eating—like tramps
    out of Beckett. (Gisela must have taken this picture;
    I'd forgotten she was there.)

            . . .

Once, the Brünings had company: three or four
    stylishly dressed women—old friends.

        There would never have been a war, they were
        still complaining, *if it wasn't for the Jews* . . .

    Gisela never commented on this visit.

            . . .

Once before I left she asked what was my
    favorite food: she would make, she
    insisted, anything I liked.
                    I was dying for
    a steak.

Was it thirty years since Gisela had prepared a steak?
    She must have cooked it over an hour (like
    cat?).
        I ate every leathery bite, while
    the Brünings munched their healthy legumes.

            . . .

Gisela packed me a lunch for the train: bread and
    sweet-butter, raisins, fresh eggs.

We shook hands warmly (she had a vigorous
    handshake: a tight squeeze, then two brisk pumps).

When I later cracked open an egg, it was
    still soft (*Gisela!*), the entire compartment
    laughing themselves to tears at my eggy mess.

    . . .

Holger's letters began to arrive at
    ever-widening intervals. He'd formed his
    own wind ensemble (photo included); was studying
    harder than ever at school.

    The last one had bad news.

Gisela had bought a car, and taught him to drive.
    They were touring; there was an accident (he
    was driving)—

    his mother had been killed.

    . . .

I can't remember the house.

I see a big, old-fashioned kitchen: on the table, bowls of
    raisins and sunflower seeds. In a cramped bedroom,
      Holger
    sleeping soundly in the next bed,
                just out of reach . . .

In one dream, I'm locked in an opera box—everyone
singing a different language. Or I'm all
alone:
window-shopping in the red-light district . . .

Gisela trying to placate her reddish frizz; brushing
the cornsilk strands out of Holger's eyes (his narrow,
ironic smile).
Herr Brüning at the breakfast table:
his pipe in his left hand—his contented,
knowing look.

There's no car. Every day we walk to the station, on our way
to a museum—Gisela preparing us for the morning's
treasures:
her arms are exclamation points; her
voice shrills with excitement . . .

But the street is blank. The house is a blank.

Why can't I picture what it *looked* like? Why should this
particular gap in my

memory disturb me so?

t w o

In the Mist

On cool, damp evenings
at the end of July,

you can walk into a mist;
and the mist

seems to disappear—
from the dirt road; from

the hill; from the trees . . .
But in the full moon,

you can begin to see it again—
it gets closer,

leaving a ring of clearness
around you, as you walk down the hill

toward the house with the light
left in the window.

House Hunting

FIRST AD. 2 fam. 10+4, 1 house off
Cambridge St., 24′ kit., 24′ master
bdrm. Low $100's.

"Fixed it all myself. Tore out some walls—
opened it all up; new tiles . . . Beautiful!
She wanted a dishwasher, I put in
a dishwasher, disposal—everything!
Beautiful!
          Thirty years we lived there . . .
                              How's
seven o'clock?"

          A waxed black Coupe de Ville
pulls up at seven sharp; he heaves himself out
on the huge upholstered door . . .
                              Small, yet stooped—
a little human question mark.
                    His short
white summer shirt at least a size too big;
his pressed, but oily, olive gabardines
bunched under his belt . . . He pastes his few, sad,

last grey hairs straight back across his freckled,
sweaty scalp.
                    (Was this the wound-up, do-it-
yourself voice on the other end of the line?)

She's even smaller. Not much younger (sixty?)
but in superior repair. Blonde; lipstick
and powder; a real figure moving under
the sheer white blouse and pink pants suit;
a Star of David—
                    (Morelli? Could *he* be
Jewish too?)

            "We moved up the North Shore
just a year ago" (her hoarse rough voice
preceding us up the narrow hallway stairs)
"when he retired. Nice place.
                    I hated leaving.
Thirty years, did he tell you? . . . time!
                                I still
can't keep him home. He misses work—but, you know,
they don't miss him . . .
                    If we stayed, it would've
killed him.
            This is the first time I've been back!"

She unlocks, and shows us in; he shows off
his handiwork: the glazed "Italian" tiles;
a dusty niche "built in for the Frigidaire."

A doll house:
            the "24' kitchen"'s just
a showroom strip of white appliances,

partitioned by two drainpipe "columns" ("Tore
out some walls") from a playpen living room . . .

Some magazines (glossy, technical) lie strewn
on the dark green, winestained wall-to-wall;

upstairs, a home computer crowds one long
(24'?) and very narrow bedroom . . .

Four—tiny?—Chinese MIT grad students
rent; a widowed sister-in-law (they don't
say whose) "has the downstairs."

                              A shade is torn;
a cardboard mobile dangles motionless.

"Look what they've done!"
                              She's shaking. "—It's
scarcely been a year! I told him we
should've cleaned it up before we took
that ad.
            I'm so ashamed. In thirty years
it's never looked like this! . . ."

                        Downstairs, it's worse—
a rabbit hole: low dusty ceilings; narrow
windows; soiled wallpaper; worn linoleum.

A labyrinth of shopping bags and cardboard
cartons stuffed with clothes. No place to move.

How long since anyone had looked down here? . . .

He doesn't say a word; she blots a tear;
I nearly hit my forehead ducking out.

We say we'll call to let them know. They know.

2

> IMMED. OCCUPANCY. Excep-
> tional high-ceilinged, fireplaced,
> lge rms, detailed woodwork, mod.
> bathrooms, 3 new kitchens, 3 story
> house plus basement & gar & park-
> ing. Make offer. Must sell.

"I'm not in real estate; I'm a lawyer—I've
got to be careful. My parents gave me this house
when I was still in law school. Now I'm tied up
in a New York deal worth over a million;
I can't waste time here. I want to sell
this weekend.
           Why do you think I'm asking
so much less than the market value? . . ."

                                        Look
at the fluted marble mantels, those intricate
ceiling medallions (hand-carved mahogany),
the high-arched Victorian windows: our own
mansion—
           and a steal—
                      with "rental units"
and a parking lot . . . Could we scrape up
a down payment?

"Four rooms here, two bathrooms;
a five-room flat—three baths—upstairs; three rooms
with bath in the attic." There's even a rusty tub
down cellar.
          Seven bathrooms? (What *was* this,
a monastery? Or a brothel—)
                              The sinks
and johns look new . . . and pasted in; a lot of
broken windows, and warped frames.

                              "Not safe?
There hasn't been a break-in since I've been here.
It's a good neighborhood—I don't know where
it gets the reputation. We've had great parties!

Don't worry about rent control. The rents
are high enough to pay your mortgage!" (He quotes
figures we like.)
                  "—Besides, they don't control
how much you can charge for parking. No one asks,
no one complains;
                  there's always a loophole . . .

                                        Look,
I've got another couple coming back tomorrow.
I don't want to pressure you (I *like* you), but
you want the house, you'll have to decide soon . . .

How much did you say you planned on putting down?"

He's not too keen about *our* figure; he wants
thirty percent—no waiting. He says
he'd even do the financing himself . . .

We'll have to make some calls tonight.
                                        Meanwhile,

we think we'd better do a little sleuthing . . .

At City Hall, the deed isn't registered
in a name we recognize (though a name we do
turns up on a lot of other properties—
whose house *is* this, anyway?)
                                        and last
changed hands less than two years ago (how long
did he say he lived there?).

                        The Rent Board says
the rents are *quite* controlled. Too controlled
to help us meet a mortgage? (How much would *we*
have to charge for parking?)
                                No one's reported
the recent plumbing and "improvements": why
didn't he want to raise the legal rent?
(What *isn't* "legal"?)

                        Our shady dream house . . .

                                                Good
we checked. Weren't we *right* to be suspicious?

But who could afford a dream house market rate,
no loopholes . . .
                Why can't we make those loopholes
work for us?

We're wasting time. Where can we
get our hands on ready cash?
                                    He said he
liked us—maybe he'll reconsider; that other
couple might be just as strapped . . .

                                    We'll call
in the morning—
                    tell him we want the house (*don't* we?)
and that we've got to find some way to work this out.

                                    3

                    SOMERVILLE. Solid 2   family
                    in   superior   location.   Cedar-
                    shingled   beauty   with   spacious
                    aptmts & contemporary updat-
                    ing, big sun deck & 2 car garage.

"They're not speaking to me upstairs. My
stepdaughter. We haven't spoken since
the Doll died last year. They even
forgot my birthday . . . Seventy-three today—
would you believe it? *Cheers!*
                                    Go on, look
around. I've got nothing to hide."

—It's oddly "tasteful" for this florid,
garrulous grandpa:
                    low-slung, plastic-covered,
blonde '50s "sectionals"; a couple of
yellow brick planters ("Built 'em myself—
not bad for an old man, eh?") fine-grained
walnut paneling; and sliding glass-door cabinets
suspended over the long oak kitchen counter . . .

The master bedroom, once evidently two ("I
knocked down that wall with my own two hands!"),
looks unslept-in . . .
                    In the spare, rumpled den,
an unmade daybed, a closetful of shirts.

A few tiles missing in the shower.

"To tell you the truth, I lost interest when
the Doll died. That's why I'm selling . . . I used to
fix up every little thing—now I don't care.
I could call my son, and move in with him
tonight—he keeps asking. Don't you believe me?
Look, I'm picking up the phone . . ."

                .   .   .

"Twenty-five years—and he's selling the house
right out from under us!
                    All my friends
live on this street; my kids' friends . . .

                            My husband
had a restaurant around the corner, three blocks
from here. It burned down two years ago—
we still haven't collected the insurance;
now he's driving a cab. We'd buy the house
ourselves if we had any money.

Who thinks they'll ever have to move . . .
                            There's so much
stuff! We've still got all the kids' toys.

At least
we won't have to pay these heating bills. Winters
it's freezing in here! This year
we were going to close off the living room
on account of the cold.
I feel sorry for anyone
moving here!

It's all his son's idea . . . If
he died, my sister and me would get half
the house; but if he sells it, he could leave
all the money to his son!

What can you do—
you have to make the best.

He drinks, did you
notice? A certified alky! Even before my
mother died . . . Believe me, he was never the
greatest husband in the world.

We get so
worried about him, alone down there . . . He's
fallen a dozen times, and he won't
let us in—thinks we're spying on him.

He just can't be trusted. Changes his mind
every five seconds—
you know, at the last minute
he could decide not to sell!

I'll be glad
to see him taken care of, though; I just hope
that son of his knows what kind of a bargain
he's getting . . .

Listen, is there any chance
you could let us stay? We've been good tenants—
fix things ourselves; always pay the rent on time . . .

Of course, it would depend on how much you were
planning to raise it. We could even squeeze in
downstairs, if you needed *our* place; put in
a daybed until my son leaves home;
                                        make do!

We've done it before . . . At least we could stay
in our own neighborhood, our own house.
                                        It would be
awful to have to move—awful to move away."

Dead-Battery Blues

The phone keeps ringing—
Somebody answer the phone!
Don't you hear it ringing?
Won't someone please pick up the phone?
It just won't stop ringing.
You know, I think nobody's home.

I can't stop talking—
You know, my tongue gets dry.
Talky-talk-talking!
My mouth's a desert, dry-bone dry.
My lips get stuck together.
It's a sin to tell a lie.

My arm won't straighten—
Can't reach that grapevine hanging there.
My fist won't open.
How? When? Why? Who? What? Where?
You know, I'm getting thirsty,
Those grapes just dangling in the air.

The engine won't turn over—
The car sits in the driveway, dead.

Plates expired.
Hubcaps missing. Tires got no tread.
Even the clock's stopped ticking.
But it's still ticking in my head.

You know, my Mama's packing—
Kansas City, here she comes.
She's going to Kansas City
(Daddy's already gone).
Her valise is heavy.
Did I say something wrong?

Old Rover's gone now—
Who'll I get to teach new tricks again.
Puss took off his boots and left me,
Left me with my only brain.
All my sweet friends are leaving.
Yesterday your letter came.

You try to wake me—
Your hand moves over my skin.
I watch you touch me,
Your fingers bony and thin.
You know, I hear you knocking,
But you can't come in.

The sun is rising—
I'm lying here on my left side.
What's tapping on the window?
Is there a pill I haven't tried?
It's starting to get light out.
It's still a little dark inside.

Crossing the Rockies

1. From the Train

At Fort Morgan, Colorado, six cars line up behind the flashing red lights
     of the railroad crossing. The deserted main street ("Main Street"?)
     disappears into a horizon of grimy snow. A small silo—Canning
     Drilling Co.—guards one side of the road.

     We won't be here long . . .

In a minute we're moving again. The next road crosses nothing
     but flat snow-fields, stretching away and back—

                                 an exercise
     in one-point perspective, except that the train keeps moving.

A clump of pastel cottages: run-down, kept-up—picturesque. A herd of
     black cattle-clusters on one dingy mound. Then
     more flat fields . . .

Our table-partner at breakfast works for a horse breeder. Arabians. He
     tells us—and we believe him—that the conglomerates
     are buying up the land:
                       "It's a conspiracy. 'Chemical farming'!—
     catches the small farmer between a rock and a hard place.

Ruins them . . . Produce drops, but the price of chemicals
keeps going up.
                    Nobody's bought a horse since the crash
last fall. The phones just stopped ringing."

Smokestacks. A cemetery with tiny snow-covered graves. The pan-piped
    grain elevators of the Denver Feed Co. (we crane our necks
    to see the tops).

A flat road runs parallel to us, just a few yards from the tracks—
    grimy cars all heading in the opposite direction.
    It's Interstate 76—the other lane barely visible beyond
    the snowy "island." One red truck keeps abreast of us,

    until we pull ahead . . .

We've lost two hours (the brakes had to be repaired in Lincoln, Nebraska).
    Our friend's train was snowbound once for twelve:
                                        "No fun,"
    he says, "A flock of pheasants was all huddled together,
    probably freezing to death . . .
                        You don't see too many
    pheasants around here, anymore."

2. *In the Rockies*

The train is so long, we can see both front and back (an extra
    engine has been added for the climb).
                            We snake our slow way
    up the windy precipice, past whitetails
    come down to forage in the softer snow.

    The Great Plains fall away . . .

Far below, telephone lines and sketchy wisps of road
    crosshatch the valley.
                Higher up, empty corrals; two houses
    that don't seem connected to anything.

    Ancient tunnels. Rickety "snowsheds," to protect the tracks
    from slides.
            Rock-filled gondola cars—abandoned
    on the rim, to break the high winds.

We wind along the edge: two feet higher every hundred feet. Even the
    clouds covering the valley are below us now.

    Ski chalets. A cluster of gray cottages, rusty
    oil barrels, and a dog.

Over the loudspeaker, the bartender alerts us to bald—or
    golden—eagles, roosting in dead trees.
                                But we
    see no eagles. The snow's getting too thick
    to see much of anything.

Neighboring peaks are suddenly steeper: we've reached the bottom
    of the higher valleys, and we're still climbing.

In the Six-Mile Tunnel ("six point two-one"), we experience the famous
    "monkey effect": "Press your noses to the windows," the bartender
    guarantees, "and you'll see the monkey."
                                We cross
    the Continental Divide . . .

Outside, it's snowing harder—trees heavy and white; telephone poles
    up to the gills in drifts.

The road below still
hasn't been cleared—a blue bus and a white pickup move
in slow motion. We deposit skiers at Fraser Winter Park:

THE ICE-BOX
OF THE NATION

50 BELOW

Sausages & Peppers (the "regional specialty") in the dining car; Muzak
with a Latin beat.
In the club-car: jagged cliffs,
jutting out like pagodas—practically scraping the car
as we squeak through (we stare straight up,
through the scenic dome).

Then down, down into the canyon
of the frozen, steaming Colorado.

3. *Problems*

No toilet.
No water: a pipe has frozen.
Flood: the water "dumps."
No heat. Outside it's below zero.
Then too much heat: it's an oven inside—someone props
the rear door of the car open. We argue.
Over the loudspeaker, the steward apologizes for his poor humor: railroad
officials had ignored his warning.
Unscheduled stop, at a suburban station: for a couple who
didn't hear the boarding announcement in Chicago (they are
not polite—the steward is shocked at their profanity).
I knock over a full glass of water. My bunk gets soaked.

Two-hour delay: in Lincoln, Nebraska, to repair the brakes.
I can't sleep in the upper berth. We argue.
Unscheduled stop: a passenger has a fit (or a slipped disc) and has to be
    helped by paramedics onto a waiting stretcher.
Unscheduled stop, outside Denver: some Saturday-night drunks
    have parked their pickup on the tracks (try finding
    a tow-truck on Sunday at 2 A.M.).
Monotony: the "regional specialty"—peppers and sausages—
    for the third day in a row.
Vexation: smokers
    in the No Smoking section.
Frustration: power failure
    at the climax of our club-car movie. We argue.
We're four hours late.
Can we ever make up the time?
Are you waiting for us at the station?
Will you still be waiting, when we arrive?
If we had a train to catch, we'd
    have already missed our connection.

4. *At the Window*

Aurora. Roseville.
"Magic City." Sweetgrass Hills.

"Where's your husband?"
"I haven't got a husband. I never married."

Winter Park ("The Ice-box of America"). Bulk Anti-freeze.
Icicle Canyon.

"John, not now, not before breakfast. I want to shake this cold."

Lovelock. Tunnel City.
Tangent. Helper.

"I hate having people do things for me, cutting my steak . . . I had a stroke—can you tell? Let's not talk about it . . . My late husband and I both came from these parts. Anyone ever tell you how the Grand Tetons got their name? (Maybe I shouldn't!) This Frenchman looked up at the mountains and said, 'What *big tits!*' "

Three Sisters Mountains. Missouri Breaks.
Diamond Peak.

"I wonder, what's the 'regional specialty' for the Donner Pass?"

Whitefish. Soda Springs.
Two Medicine River.

"I crossed the head of that river—and the mouth."

Osceola. Ottumwa.
Winnemucca. Truckee.

"I built that bank . . . the building . . . my firm did."

Floor Systems Repair. Kish & Sons Electric.
Sparks.

"We're the Crook twins, C-R-O-O-K . . . just like the word."

Commerce City. Nugget Casino and Hotel.
Price.

Child (playing *Trivial Pursuits*): "What's the President's official theme song?"
Mother: " 'We're in the Money!' "

"Pig Capital of the World." "Smelt Capital of the World."
"Lumber Capital of the U.S." "Egg Capital of the World."
"Apple Capital of the World."

"I'm a Congressman—retired. I could've run again if I wanted to. Too much flying back and forth, though. I don't fly anywhere anymore unless I have to. That's why I voted against the airline appropriation . . ."

Trojan Nuclear Power Plant. Koch Oil Refinery.
"Biggest Little City in the World."

". . . It's the Weimar Republic!"

Geneva. Havre.
Malta. Glasgow.

"We're both retired. Well, I've been retired all my life. We're newlyweds, actually—just celebrating our first anniversary."

Fort Union (new time zone). *Grand Junction.*

"You should go at Mardi Gras."
"That's what everyone tells me—but I get so nervous in crowds."

Izaak Walton Inn. Polish Museum.
Emigrant Gap. Blackfeet Indian Writing Co.

"Come from Alaska. Ketchikan. Goin' to Florida . . . Son's in Florida. Lake Okeechobee . . . Got some time on my hands—do a little fishin'—meet people, talk to people . . ."

The Bar of America. Saint James Hotel.
Frank Pure Food Company (Franksville). ZELDA'S DINER: OPEN.

5. The Train at Night

It's dark and the relentless forward movement makes you feel
    disconnected and lonely

But it's smooth and the endless rocking
    cradles you

Even the rumbling comforts you—even the rain
    streaking across the window

Even when the rain turns to sleet

Distant lights, outlines of trees—going by at
    different speeds

The headlights of one car, a neon
    bar sign

ELECTRICAL SUPPLY   RR CROSSING   MOBIL   MOTEL

The streetlights of one main street, a dimly lit station, maybe
    a stop and someone—an elderly woman with
    a suitcase—getting on

Where are we? The dark window
    shows you only your own face peering out

Then moving again—the bell clanging at the crossing like
    a fire bell, a dinner bell—the froggy
    train whistle replying

Not to worry

A darker rumbling—we're over water now—then moving
   faster and even more quietly

   further into it

three

Fourteen People

(after a portrait series by Ralph Hamilton)

Ralph Hamilton

It's all in the eyes. The broad, smudged,
helpless body shivers and dissolves, washing out
its thin, coloring-book outlines; arms hang
stiff at the sides; vest (popped?) open; broad
white tie tight under a shovel of red beard;
feet apart, planted—barely—in Japanese sandals.
(An "aesthetic" touch? or homey, summery—
countering the long-sleeved Windsor formality?)
But the eyes: coal-blue, white-hot, sapphire coals,
shifting behind the flat front of flesh—
untouchable; unshakable . . .
                              The disappearing artist
keeping close behind the flimsy painted cardboard
with holes poked out only for the eyes.

Lloyd Schwartz

Something behind the philosophical glasses' glass
draws one in; the whole "look" centripetal—
condensing, concentrating, the head a small nebula,
"nebulous" in its rusty cloud of hair and beard.
While the *art nouveau* body—high-necked, courtly—
pretty shaky, really; hardly a leg to stand on,
brushed—as they are—out from under, centrifugally,
into the surrounding swirl; hands hanging on
to each other (fused, practically) for dear life . . .
Outside (wasn't this painted indoors?) it's all gray.
A storm's coming, or going. His lips are trembling.
Cold? But his collar's open, trousers summer-white.
The storm's inside—if there is a storm.
Something in the eyes has nothing to do with weather.

Gail Mazur

The knowing eye, barely perceptible under dark shades;
a radiant magenta jacket, loosely knotted over
billowing, shimmery "cerulean" pants; dark hair pouring
over delicate, sexy shoulders. A celebrity? A star?
What's the joke she's almost keeping to herself?
And yet, one hand (girlishly, nervously) clutches a finger
of the other. And, aren't the shoulders slightly "pinched"?
Knees too close? And the smile, uncertain? The dark glasses
forbidding? Her face crossed by too many shadows . . .
She wants to—she wants *us* to—step back, step back
and see her shine (she is shining). She wants
room to shine.
              While that wide eye, that shadowed eye, sees
into the dark, sees a dark her own beams can't reach.

Frank Bidart

"I look like I've had a spike driven down the back
of my head!" And he accepts it, this picture,
likes it. It's him, though the jaw and lips
have been smeared downward; the brow, the eyes
knotted, unwilling to alter their gaze.
The sloping, bewildered shoulders anticipate—and give
in to—their mysterious, wearying burden.
Collar open; jacket open; hands empty, and open.
He makes his way through a thick fog, through
the canvas—toward us; wearing, like the air itself,
the bleak color of earth. How much sorrow can he stand,
this night-walker, before he can't separate himself
from his sorrow? . . . this ghost, this pale, empty-handed
monster, stumbling forward with his monstrous grief.

Jane Struss

> *Now the sun rises, rises so bright,*
> *As if no misfortune had come in the night.*
> *Misfortune has come, come only to me—*
> *But the sun shines for all, for all to see.*

The spotlight is so bright I can hardly see;
but haven't I seen enough already? My mother
an alcoholic, a suicide; my son retarded;
marriage a joke; my Cinderella daughter
farmed out by her next mother to strangers.
Some of this I chose—losing that wasting world
to sing Orpheus; Dido's lament, and Phaedra's—
a woman's love and life; the death of children;

songs of a wayfarer; the song of the Earth.
My suburban Dorabella was a fiasco (I tried
to stab myself with a spoon!). Pathetic at comedy,
with tragedy I'm right at home: serious songs,
the skull under the skin. Look at my eyes—
see what I have seen; see what I see. Listen!

Mr. and Mrs. Hamilton

They're quite a pair. He's the quiet one—
the Scottish side; though the two or three times
he lost his temper, his rage was terrifying.
He's so shaky now . . . Most evenings he'll sit home
watching something—hockey, or baseball—on TV
and won't open his mouth, except for his nightcap.
She'll come charging in, stand in front of the set,
tell him something, sit down with a huge sigh
or groan, doze off (I've mostly painted her asleep),
get up, go out to the kitchen, spread a couple of
thick pats of butter on a piece of white bread
(the French side), come back with a diet soda,
and collapse into a chair with another heaving sigh.
At the end of the movie, she'll wake up
and go to bed upstairs. He'll sleep on the couch.

Neither one was ever particularly affectionate.
He's so bottled up; she so loud, so aggressive.
Once, when I was little, I came up behind where
she was sitting, and threw my arms around her.
She jumped three feet into the air! She thought
I was going to kill her; I had nightmares for weeks.
Now she's retired too, and things at home are even

more difficult. She got me so mad, I had to
put off painting her for a month—I was afraid
I might be unfair. Though this time, I think
I've almost captured her—her energy; her power.
People tell me *he's* my best subject, my most
touching. Ten years ago, his shadow had my profile;
now all our portraits have the same shadow.

Joyce Peseroff

"Look at that yellow shirt!" "Banana." "No . . . *canary;*
and those vanilla slacks." "Slack? That hard crease
could hold her up." "Neat; perfect posture. But easy,
comfortable—shirt out, short sleeves, earth shoes,
that mushroom-cloud of hair . . ." "What about those buttons—
all buttoned; and her arms at attention, one foot forward.
I bet she's itching for a fight . . ." "Or ready for one;
I wouldn't mess with those laser slit-eyes." "But where's
her face? It seems . . . unfinished; almost un-formed."
"She wants it that way: for surprises." "Or secrets . . ."
"Her lips ("Lips? *Where?*" "Don't be funny.") are sealed.
She has to be wary." "*Chary* . . . She won't give an inch."
"She can't—she's on an edge. There's nothing behind her."
"Not about to fall though." "No, unassailable." "Scary . . ."

Robert Pinsky

        ". . . that rarest category of talents, a poet-critic."

Demonstrating this talent *vis-à-vis* your portrait, as in
      your wicked
"light-eating silence" parody ("composed in less time than
      it takes
to type"), you went straight for the jugular: the "tense
      jaw,"
"iron smile," and "mask-like" face. I'd found it sweeter—
      innocent white
and blue (short sleeves and jeans); round brown eyes averted
      in athletic
humility; a touch, maybe, of the tennis-court conqueror's
      acknowledgment
of adulation; but more Greek bronze (*kouros*) than bronzed
      Berkeley prince.

You've often bent your irony toward yourself. Who else would
      crack jokes
about calling his next book by his first name? Is this pose
      putting on
what enemies take you for: All-American (Jewish) Success?
      Lucky S.O.B.
waiting for the prizes to roll in? Success, friends agree,
      suits you—
though it's been painting you further up the ladder from
      reach.
Your "mask" tells what vigilance against fatigue, distraction,
      discouragement
the competitor maintains, to protect his skill, his sanity, and
      his art.

Margo Lockwood

"The Melancholy Life-of-the-Party," her familiar rosy flush
muted here, transmogrified into Watteau's hapless, quizzical
Italian Comedian . . . pearl-pale Pierrot, in white Commedia smock.
Black Irish, though, the glint and head-tilt. Black eyebrow
up for all the latest (jokes, poems, gossip); dark, roving eye
out, casting for the day's trouble. Tight-lipped, downcast heroine
of her own Pearl White cliffhanger: WIDOWED MOTHER OF FOUR
AND THE MORTGAGE DUE . . . Breathless, hairbreadth, in-one-door-
out-the-other escape-artist star of that long-running farce,
The Horse in the Attic, her failing Brookline bookshop (also with a
storied past). At the hard-core tail end of a Cambridge party,
belting Cole Porter, lounge-style: "What's the good of swank, or
cash in the bank galore?" GROUCHO, CHICO, HARPO . . . AND MARGO,
bowing out with this week's latest, un-secret word: "Fuckoleum!"

Tom Joanides

Which of these statements is true?

(a) I just got off the boat from Albania; (b) I look like
I just got off the boat from Albania; (c) I'm a master potter,
baking porcelains in a kiln I built myself; (d) I'm a master
pastry chef, sampling desserts I bake for a famous
downtown hotel; (e) I live on donuts, sometimes one or two
dozen at a time; (f) I'm a diet freak, starving myself
on tofu and brown rice, purging my system with gallons of warm
salted water; (g) I'm an actor—a good one; (h) I've played an
amazing joke: I came home with someone I'd just met, went
into the bathroom, and shaved off my beard; (i) All my clothes
come from Goodwill; (j) I drive a Mercedes; (k) I'm the
artist's oldest friend; (l) I'm unhappy, I hate my life; (m)
Everything changes—give me a minute; (n) None of this is true.

"Artie" Matteosian

This one's my favorite. It's so loving: the generous pink dress,
silver-white hair, rose-thin lipstick . . . painted with such care.
Those subtle white lines—guidelines?—mapping her face and neck.
("I had to be dragged in to pose; then dragged back to see it.
I didn't want to be painted. I had on a zebra-striped dress
that made me look like an awning; thank God he changed it.")
Her "carriage," the humble way she's got both hands in front of her
holding her glasses. ("So professional! As if I'd been called away
from my desk; which I *was*. Not that I have to work; I'd go crazy
without something to do, something useful, to get me through the day.")
And her eyes, her *eye*—so forthright, and sad; as if she'd seen
something, and can't say what it is, or look away. Her other eye
already obliterated in its shadow. ("I don't know, I don't know
anything. Why would anyone want to paint me? Who'd want to look?")

Danny and Mary Kelleher

Your intimidating teacher—bald; birdlike; bell-bottomed;
double-shirted (no longer the fashion). Crossed arms; piercing,
imperious eyes (some things never change). The lines in his face
glaring white neon . . . *She's* changed. Where's the caustic
blond pixie (his precocious student)? Sketch-pad wild with color—
jungles of animals, sexual landscapes. Later, sparrow skeletons
and dead mice, drawn from life; half-worked poems; elementary
guitar; tarot cards and bird mask (ominous, home-made). Not yet
this waif, waiting by the eternal roadside—a glittering, low-
necked cocktail dress half-hidden under her sagging carcoat.

Remember the late-Sunday-afternoon wine and gossip? The kids into
everything—the encyclopedia; the refrigerator; the conversation.

(Who's knifing Who in the cutthroat art marketplace? Who got
the grant *you* deserved?) The walls generously hung with students
and friends (some already "names"). His own outsize
ethereal abstractions stashed in a hallway—too big to put up,
or give away. Remember what confusion when one actually sold?

When was it they moved to the further suburbs? Decided to adopt
a "troubled teenager"? The nuclear family, detonating:
midnight hospital rushes (the youngest's asthma; an older one's
arm, shredded); stalled cars, and salaries; studios abandoned.

He was your best, your toughest teacher. Her vivid pastels
even you were willing to trade your paintings for.

They wanted to be artists, and people. We used to visit them . . .

Now they're frescoes. Earthy, luminescent greens and browns,
pale pre-Renaissance skin, fleshed from the muddy plaster;
unhappy, fallen Adam and Eve; a disapproving Angel delivering
merciless Annunciations to his sullen, empty-eyed Madonna.

four

Goodnight, Gracie

for Gracie Allen, 1906–1964

"Almost everything I know today I learned by listening to
myself when I was talking about things I didn't under-
stand."

"Mrs. Burns, I love that zany character of yours."
"So do I, or else I wouldn't have married him."

"You mean you understand it?"
"Well, of course! When I misunderstand what you say, I al-
ways know what you're talking about."

Home very late from a Hollywood party, George and Gracie
can hear their phone ringing, but can't find the key
to get in. George is vexed, and tired, but Gracie is dying
to wake Blanche Morton next door and gossip about dancing
with Gary Cooper: "His belt buckle ruined my gardenia!"
Soon the Mortons are locked out ("Gracie, did you close
the door?" "No, but I will!"); the locksmith's tools locked in
(will his jealous new wife ever believe this?); and the
phone never stops . . . Day breaks, and George breaks in
through a window. "I've got a wonderful idea," he announces.

"From now on, we'll leave a door-key under the mat." "But I put one there *months* ago," Gracie argues, "and we couldn't get in last night." The telephone again: who's been trying to get through? "Gracie, who was on the phone?" "I was."

· · ·

"It's not a matter of whether I'm right or wrong—it's a matter of principle."

"Men are so deceitful. They look you right in the eye while they're doing things behind your back."

"Don't rush me. It isn't easy to make up the truth."

Ronnie's dying for a part in a new play whose famous author is fascinated by Gracie; but the only role still open is intended for a middle-aged actress, sole support of her widowed mother . . . "I'm a widow too," Gracie fibs, "and Ronnie supports me!" Smitten, the playwright invites her to dine in his room. "My husband died in a shipwreck," she embroiders, "on our honeymoon." "Lucky you survived!" "Oh, I wasn't there." In breezes Ronnie, and asks for "Dad." Gracie (thinking fast): "He can never forget his father." Playwright (bewildered): "But he never knew him." Gracie (triumphant): "If he knew him, he'd forget him!" Enter "the Widow Morton" with Ronnie's long-lost father, to unravel Gracie's tangled web . . . Blushing, the playwright offers Ronnie a part; Ronnie's in heaven; Gracie's forgiven; the playwright, like George himself, resigned to applaud her irresistible assassinations.

· · ·

"I may not be here long."
"Where are you going?"
"Oh, don't I wish I knew!"

"I didn't think people felt this wonderful when they were going. But, then again, this is the first time I've gone."

"If you ask me a question and I don't answer, don't be nervous. Just take your hats off."

. . . how casually we treated Gracie's illness. Those pills made me feel very secure. I figured we could go on this way year after year—it never entered my mind that anything would change it. Then one evening Gracie had another one of her attacks. I gave her the pill, we held on to each other—but this time it didn't work. When the pain continued, I called Dr. Kennamer, and they rushed Gracie to the hospital. . . . Two hours later Gracie was gone.

"He's crazy about dancing. His new wife has got to be a
very good dancer." Gracie thinks she's dying—having opened
by mistake Harry von Zell's telegram meant to save George
from a weekend seasick on his sponsor's yacht: EXAMINED YOUR
WIFE CONDITION SERIOUS URGE YOU DO NOT LEAVE HER . . . "I'm a
very sick woman, but my health is so good, I didn't even know it!"
She's had three agencies send over their most attractive
candidates to replace "the late Mrs. Burns": "Sounds like it
won't be easy to fill *her* shoes." "What size do you wear?"
"How old was she when she passed on?" "Well, I'd rather not say—
she hasn't passed on far enough for that." George, however,
has already chosen his next wife, who—relieved, reprieved—
would rather George hadn't explained: "It's such a letdown. After
this, how can I be gay about an ordinary thing like living?"

L o v e

"Why live? I never really thought.
I never went to church, or read books.
I worked, for a railroad; but work
was like sleepwalking.
I took drugs and drove around.
I married a girl who loved me.
Why? I wasn't very good to her
most of the time. And she died."

"I wasn't very pretty, or 'bright.'
School meant nothing, I couldn't wait
till it was over. After graduation,
I went to work for my father.
I needed to get out.
I can remember a fight about a car;
I wanted one so badly, and they knew
it was so I could be with him."

"Sometimes I felt grateful—even if she
was a little overweight;
I wasn't such a winner myself.
We broke up a couple of times. I
hit her once, when we were stoned . . .

After we got married, I had myself dried out.
We got more serious. We were even
planning to get married again in church."

"Things got better after he got
off the drugs. Things also
didn't change. Friday night: bowling, or a
hockey game. Saturday: a movie, double date.
Sunday: my parents, who were beginning
to 'accept the situation.'
Nothing happened; only sometimes
it happened more peacefully."

"What could I do? She was already dead
in the ambulance. Never sick a day
in her life! Who could believe this?
I knew they'd blame me. No one said a word;
but I knew.
Everyone said it was terrible—
but that I was young; I should be patient;
I'd get over it."

"I felt dizzy . . . We were in the kitchen,
talking, while I was making dinner
(I was a terrible cook).
I said I was feeling dizzy. It was getting
harder to breathe. I remember falling,
and him leaning over me, saying my name,
asking what's the matter? I remember thinking
someone should turn off the stove."

"I put my flower on her casket,
like everyone else. Even the priest
was upset. She was so young!

He asked me to come and see him . . .
Nobody could know what we felt.
I don't think I knew myself.
All I could think was
I wanted to be with her—inside."

     "Why did you do it?"
     "I had to be with you."

     "You were so young."
     "I couldn't wait."

     "You were alive . . ."
     "The world was a coffin."

     "Did it hurt much?"
     "I don't remember, now."

Accomplice

Getting out
after reading, or writing,
late—

or was it waiting
for a call?

—past the windows where,
on hot nights,
they don't pull all
the shades all
the way down . . .

(I walk by slowly, twice.)

Then up a darker, more
private street.
My footsteps echo.
Echo? Someone else's feet,
the nightwatchman—
he greets me
with a wave of his flash:

"Hot night!"
"I know it."

"Out for a walk?"
"Too hot inside."

"Cooler inside
than out . . ."

He points to the upper windows
of one of those
gray frame campus buildings
he's guarding:

"Cooler up there . . . Want to
go up?"

He's asked me before.

I put my arm on his shoulder
(he grins), cup
his ear, and whisper:

"What if
somebody caught us?"

"Who'd be out
this time of night?"

"But it's dark . . ."

He elbows me:
"We don't need any light!"

—A noise. Flap-flap-flap . . .
Footsteps? The flash:

>*"Hands up! I gotcha covered."*
>*"Don't shoot, I'm innocent!"*

The light falls on a boy—in sneakers,
khakis, open khaki shirt.

He laughs; the old man guffaws:

>"You know what we do
>to people who break the law?"
>(He winks at me.) "We take them up
>to that little room up there,
>and show them what's what . . ."

>"I know," the boy says.
>"But don't get so excited;
>you know, I thought I
>heard something moving
>in the corner building."

>"Uh-oh, I'd better check.
>Don't go 'way!"

We watch the watchman. We're in
no hurry. We stay.

He stands there . . . a hand on his hip,
the other fingering
the buttons of his open shirt:

"What are you doing
out so late?"
"Just walking around."

"Where do you live,
around here?"
"Not far."

"In school?"
"Sort of. You?"

"Not really."
"Then what are *you* up to?"

"Locked out," he says. "Said
I'd be home early.
—Hey, wait here, I have to pee."

He goes behind the house; I watch him
standing with his back to me.

Then he's out of sight . . .

—A crash.
Broken window?

"Hey, watch out!" (No sound.)
"You OK?" (No answer.)

A thud. Muffled rustling through the bushes.
I look around—carefully.

"Where are you?" I whisper.
"What are you doing? What's going on?"

"Shsh!" (He's breathless.)
"—Where do you live? I'll walk you home."

"What happened?"

"Must've stepped on some glass.
—Hey, let's go
before the old guy comes back."

He's off—I follow;
he knows the way . . .

I let him in.

        "What's down there?"

        "The cellar."
        "Let's see!"

At the bottom of the stairs
a long, damp
cement corridor—
shadeless lightbulbs,
padlocked doors . . .

        "—That's enough.
        Let's get out of here!"

He swings up the stairs,
and disappears.

                    2

By the end of summer,
he's a fixture—

knocks at all hours,

sometimes talks until he
falls asleep in a chair.

It seems he's run away—
is on probation;
hasn't reported recently.

Calls his mother every day;
every day
she threatens to turn him in.

> "She'd turn me in for a nickel.
> —You wouldn't do
> that, would you?"

He makes friends in the building . . .

I start keeping
beer for him; sit up
and worry
when a night goes by
without a visit:

> "Where were you yesterday?"
> "You sound like my mother."
> "Well . . . where *were* you?"

> "Look at this!" he says one day—

slipping a hunting knife
from its sheath at his hip:

"Feel the weight! What do
you think of that blade?"

"I'm impressed . . . But what
do you want with *that*?"

"It's for you."

"For me? What for?"

"You don't take
care of yourself enough."

"But what would I *do* with it?"

"I don't know,"

he looks down
at the knife in my hand:

"The world is rough . . ."

One night he's really jumpy:

"Come with me,
I want to show you something!"

I follow him down
into the cellar . . .

He swings open a closet, pushes
aside some rolls of paper—

"What's *that*?"

"What does
it look like?"

"What's it doing here?"

"I brought it."

"Why did you bring it *here*?"

"Where else
would I put it?"

"Where did you get it?"

"What difference
does that make?"

"IT MAKES A DIFFERENCE."

"Why?"

I don't know what to answer.
I look away . . .

"Is this why
you come here?"

"Why do you think?"

He watches me closely, then
puts a hand on my shoulder
and pulls me closer—

his mouth almost touches my ear:

"What's the matter? Aren't we
friends? I thought you liked me . . .

—Hey, why are you
looking at me like that?

What are you going to do?"

I take hold of his arm . . .

"DON'T!"

He backs into the stairway, stumbles,
turns, and scrambles up the steps.

"—Wait!"

He doesn't come back.

3 Epilogue

A copying machine, and two typewriters,
are found in the cellar closet.
No one can figure out
how they got there.

A man on my floor I hardly knew
confesses he lost fifty dollars
"bailing out that kid who
used to hang around here . . ."

A friend staying over
is surprised to discover
a hunting knife—lying among the utensils
in a kitchen drawer.

Pseudodoxia Epidemica

It is evident not only in the general frame of Nature, that things most manifest unto sense have proved obscure unto the understanding.

Sir Thomas Browne

"Hi."
"Hi."

"You OK?"
"I guess . . . You?"

"I miss you."
"I miss you too."

"What are you doing?"
"Reading . . . You?"

"*The Late Show.*"
". . . What time will you be home?"

"Around dinner. Eat out?"
"I guess."

"The movie's starting."
"Thanks for calling."

"See you tomorrow."
"See you."

·

Sorry I won't be here when you
get home. I need time to think. Please
don't try to reach me—I'll keep calling
till I reach you, to explain.
                    Don't worry!

                        Love

> *The common opinion of the Oestridge, or Sparrow-
> Camel, conceives that it digesteth Iron; and this is con-
> firmed by the affirmations of many; beside swarms of
> others.*

"Hi,
it's me . . ."

"Where are you?"
"I'd rather not say."

"Why aren't you here?"
"I'll tell you when I see you."

"When?"
"Whenever you want."

"Now."

". . . Are you angry?"
"I'll tell you when I see you."

> *Moles are blind, and have no eyes.*

"—How could you
do this to me?"

"Do you want me to come back?"

"I'm so angry, I could
kill you!"

"Do you want me to come back?"

"No! Yes.
—How could you do this to me?"

"Do you want me to come back?"

> Concerning the Chameleon, there generally passeth an
> opinion that it liveth only upon air.

"I'm sorry . . . Do you
believe me? I'm really sorry—
I didn't want to hurt you; I just
didn't care."

". . . But why do you want to see me?"

"Sometimes, I just like
to be with you."

"I like to be with you too."

". . . You do?"
"Yes."

In every place we meet with the picture of the Pelican,
opening her breast with her bill and feeding her young
ones with the blood distilling from her.

L—dear
I tried to find
the list with Michael's
number on it to call you
because I was worried—
Please have pity on me
I do a lot of really wrong things
—but have very little
pity on myself

C

A Loadstone, held in the hand, doth either cure or give
great ease in the Gout, or as an amulet it also cureth the
head-ache; for perceiving its secret power to draw mag-
netical bodies, men have invented a new attraction, to
draw out the dolour and pain of any part.
                                                        And there-
fore upon this stone they graved the Image of Venus.

The further away you get, the more I need you:

the further away I get you, the more you need.
The further away I need you, the more you get:

the further away you need, the more I get you.

The more I get you, the further away you need:

the more you get, the further away I need you.
The more you need, the further away I get you:

the more I need you, the further away you get.

Simple Questions

Can you hear me? Do you
understand?

How are you feeling? Can you
feel anything?

Are you in pain? Is there anything
I can do?

Do you know me? Do you
know who I am?

.

When I dream about my father, he's
recovered. Home. He can move—walk; talk to
my mother; complain; even argue.
(The doctor at the hospital, not encouraging,
wouldn't deny this possibility.)

He comes downstairs and makes his way
toward his favorite chair, the one
with the florid cushions he'd stitched himself.

His breath comes hard, as it had
in the hospital; but suddenly, miraculously—

better!

I started having this dream
after my first visit.

               •

"What comes after seven? Say it.
Try! What's the number after seven? . . . That's

right! Now what comes after eight? Tell me,
what comes after eight? . . ."

Once my mother got him to count
to fifteen.

Then, seven.

               •

He was the old man you'd pass as you
hurried down the corridor to see your friend
in traction (touch football
terpsichore), or with pneumonia (not, thank God,
critical); the old man with the sucked-in
yellow face, no teeth, the oxygen tube
up his nose, the urine sac hanging from his bed.
Breathing hard; hardly moving; his eyes
blank, yet (weren't they?) following you . . .

Not your own.

The unhappy family whose
trouble he was . . .

NOT YOUR OWN.

·

"Hello! Say hello. How do you
feel? Are you feeling better?"

"A little better."

"Good." She leans over and
looks into his face. "Did you sleep OK?"

No answer.

"Do you know me? Who
am I? What's my name?"

"M-mom."

"And what's your name? Can you
tell me your name?"

"Sam."

"Good! Are you hungry? Let me give you
some soup? A little custard? . . ."

"No."

"Are you thirsty? Where's your straw?
Would you like some juice?"

"Yes."

"How about a nice shave? Would you
like me to give you a shave? . . . There!

Now you look handsome!"

He rubs his face with his right hand;
he keeps rubbing his face.

•

"Are you the son? What a pity! He seems like
such a nice person, such a sweet old man.
It's a shame . . . Last night he was very quiet—
slept like a baby. Didn't bother anybody!
By the end of the week he'll be ready to go home."

•

"Wake up! Open your eyes. Can you
keep your eyes open?"

No answer.

"Look at me. Can you see me? Who
am I? Do you know who I am?"

No answer.

"Can you hear me? Do you understand
what I'm saying to you?"

". . . Yes."

"Look around. Where are you?
Do you know where you are?"

No answer.

"Can you feel anything? Can you feel
my hand? Where's my hand?"

I put my hand in his; he
squeezes hard.

"Who am I? Do you know who I am?"

". . . Yes."

"What's my name? Say it. Who
am I? Tell me who I am."

". . . Fa-ther."

                    •

No love lost. A lifetime of
anger; resentment; disapproval. Could I pretend—
even now—a deep, personal concern?

Prodding him to speech (what the doctor
ordered), to recover enough of his mind to
help my mother endure his release,

hypnotized me, gripped my attention, the way
his right hand gripped my hand—the last remnant
of his unrelenting, fist-clenched

denunciations of the world:

of the "Hitler Brothers," who refused him even
a moment's rest in the sweatshops where he
spent his working life stitching men's clothes;

of relatives, or neighbors, never generous or
grateful enough, for someone rarely generous
or grateful; of my friends, of *me*—stymied by my

anger; resentment; disapproval . . . The way
his right hand gripped the hedgecutter, lifted it,
and aimed it at my head.

"I have to go now. Goodbye! I'll see you
tomorrow . . . Do you hear me?
Feel better. I hope you feel better."

                    •

"How do you feel? Talk to me. Tell me
how you feel."

". . . Not so good."

"Are you in pain? Where does
it hurt you?"

No answer.

"Can I do anything? Should I
get the doctor?"

". . . No doctor can cure me."

                    •

"He had a restless night; couldn't swallow—
we had to pump out his throat. His pressure
sank way down. There was nothing else we
could do . . . I'm sorry. He just fell
asleep, very peaceful, and stopped breathing."

•

"Can you hear me?"
"Yes."

"How are you feeling?"
"A little better."

"Do you know me? Who am I?"
"My son."

"Is there anything I can do?"
"No."

Vermeers

WHY I LOVE VERMEER

1. Power.

When I moved to my new house, I thought I'd lost all my Vermeer books. I was frantic for days. How could I have lost track of them "even for the least division of an hour"? Even the most inadequate reproduction (and they're *all* inadequate) has the power to move me. Lately, though, merely looking at them hasn't seemed enough. But what more can one do? What more do they *want*? What are they going to ask of me now?

2. Personal reasons.

The women in the paintings—opening a window, reading a letter, pouring milk, holding a glass of wine—remind me, in their eyes, their smiles (giving, inward), their "centeredness," remind me of certain people I love; especially (this gets more complicated), especially my mother.

3. Profundity.

Their network of contradictions (clarity and mystery; reticence and bravura; heroism and humility—not necessarily a contradiction) suggests an intelligence, an inner life, beyond the other "little" Dutch masters—and equal, it seems to me, in its way, to the nakedness and tragedy of Rembrandt. "Rembrandt ist Beethoven," I heard an old woman say to herself in the Rijksmuseum, "Vermeer ist Mozart." Why must one choose either over the other?

4. *Rarity.*

So few survive (thirty-six, fewer than the number of Shakespeare plays; and one attribution has recently been called into question). Each one—taken in, loved for itself—calls into mind each of the others.

5. *Inaccessibility.*

The summer of the great retrospective in Europe (including all the Vermeers still in private collections), I had to go. Obsessed, I kept traveling to see as many more as I could. In Germany, I lied to get into a closed museum. At what wouldn't I stop?

6. *Accessibility.*

I grew up in New York, which has more Vermeers (eight) than any other city in the world. Any other *country* (there are only seven in Holland). I've never lived in a city without a Vermeer.

1. THE CONCERT

Three figures:

A girl in silver folds of satin—
                              a puff
of yellow sleeve; hair-ribbons. A large pearl

floating at her visible ear; pearls
circling her neck. Her eyes fixed on the keyboard—
cast down, concentrating . . .

A man in brown—
                    his back to us; thick curls
draping his heavy shoulders. A lute in his lap,
his fingers lightly touching the stops—
one foot braced against the base of the harpsichord;
his narrow scabbard scraping the tiles . . .

A woman standing—
                    pregnant, in a morning jacket
(blue velvet, ermine-trimmed); hair severely brushed.
Lips parting; eyes lowered to the music
wrinkled in her fingers. One hand open, raised
in keeping time; in benediction. *Pearls* . . .

Shadows surround the light surrounding them.

In the dim foreground,
                    a monstrous table
draped with a heavy red rug; open pages
grazed by the pearly light; a lute. A huge viol
lying (half-hidden) on the marbled tiles:
black; white; black; black; black . . .

On the far wall,
                    above the girl's head,
hanging from a nail, a dark landscape—
darkly framed. Above the harpsichord (sunlit
Arcadia painted on its open lid),
a darker picture—

three figures:

A turbaned crone demanding the heavy coin
her shadowy client tenders in his fingers, his arm
circling the bare shoulder of a young woman
laughing—head thrown back, her eye fixed on his;
one breast exposed; her fingers strumming a lute.

2. Young Woman Putting on Pearls

What do we see first?

A free-standing, radiant girl—
                                her healthy arms
lifted to pull the yellow ribbon-ends
of her pearl choker tightly into a knot;
her fur-trimmed lemon-velvet sleeves
pushed up past her elbows; her serious smile . . .

A faded yellow curtain—pushed aside—admits
a rush of light that sets the flat gray wall
we face (the whole canvas) trembling with detail:
the tiny pearls; a feathery powder-duster; the
rosy ribbon dangling from her tight chignon . . .

Calmly dazzled (like us), she makes
                              her offering to
the light: the necklace; the large teardrop
pearl weighing heavily upon her ear; her face itself.
The light accepts—bestows—yet warns her back, back
across the room from the mirror she gazes into . . .

All that light,

casting dark things—the blue ("Prussian") cloth
(a cloak?) heaped on the table, the gilt
cosmetic-box, the black porcelain vase (Chinese?)
hidden in its folds, a chair in a corner
we can barely make out—deeper into shadow . . .

> *Happiness here is simply a matter of*
> *being visible.*

> *Vanity of vanities, saith the Preacher;*
> *all is vanity.*

> *This is one of the few Vermeer paintings in*
> *perfect condition.*

3. OFFICER AND LAUGHING GIRL

"Who is this man? I can barely
make out his face in the window-glare.
A fierce silhouette. The glowing edge
of his floppy, broad-brimmed hat—
the Devil with a halo! His
red jacket on fire. An assault
of maleness; a mystery . . .

Does he see my terror?

—Or is he staring at the map
on the wall behind me? Or out the

open window? His impatient hand
on his hip, even sitting down.
What does he keep staring at? What
makes him stay?"

·

"Why doesn't she just drink her wine
and relax? She looks like she's
about to cry. I can see the tears
welling up. But no—her eye
is clear. Her hands on the table,
around her glass, palms up—ready to take
whatever is given . . .

What do I have to give?

—I could travel past the edge
of the known world, and never find
a pearl worthy of this smile
that sees right through me,
sees my darkness—
yet doesn't cease to smile."

4. THE ARTIST IN HIS STUDIO

In the Museum of the History of Art
(where art is history, history

art), an artist

sitting at his easel—turned from us—
begins to paint his muse:

History, who holds to her bosom
an enormous Book—

her eyes drawn down to it, down . . .

In one hand, she balances
an antique trumpet, instrument of

annunciation—the annunciation
of the artist's place in history:

his "Fame." A large map

on the wall—his place in the world;
a gleaming brass chandelier, no candles;

light pouring in from some unseen source . . .

He wears an outdated, comical outfit—
pantaloons

and puffed sleeves (striped black and white);
red stockings; a black beret.

He bears a peculiar resemblance
to a mysterious, isolated figure

in other Vermeer paintings:

The Procuress (Dresden); *Couple with a
Wine Glass* (Brunswick);

just as the girl in blue
might be someone in another museum.

Her head is crowned with laurel.
He can't turn his eyes from her . . .

Filling the space between them, a table
strewn with props: long silks; an open

sketchbook, hanging
limply over the edge; a giant mask,

in a shaft of light . . . face up.
—Whose face?

Behind a chair, an opulent tapestry
(blue leaves; unreadable browns

and golds), drawn aside, allowing us to
view the scene:

       the canvas in the painting

       still nearly bare—the artist beginning
       to paint the laurel wreath . . .

5. Woman Holding a Balance

What is she weighing? Gold
in burnished piles, scattered pearls—

against the Resurrection and the Life?

Or is this, as the legend says, only a test
to divine the sex of her unborn child? . . .

Light edges in from behind the curtains,

over her face, her fingers
from which the delicate scales depend.

On the wall behind her, the Last Judgment looms,
the hysterical world of the spirit . . .

She balances herself,

touching the edge of the table before her;
the shadowy things of this world

reach toward her hand . . .

Next to the covered window, a sliver of
mirror; if she looked up, she could see what is

there to see—

> *her face; the gold; the pearls;*
>
> *the light;*
> *the resurrection and the life.*

five

In the Jewish Cemetery
in Queens

A stone's throw from my uncle's grave—
my uncle Joe, who died four days
before the market crashed, of
pemphligus, incurable skin disease—

> BELOVED HUSBAND AND
> OUR FATHER
> JOSEPH SINGER
> Age 35 years

—fruit-and-vegetable man who left
four thin kids and a wife
who spent every last thin hope
on finding him a cure: ears stuck out,

bug-eyed—*handsome*—on the stiff
enamel photo stuck to the black
granite: tree-shaped, branches
lopped off, to show his youth . . .

A stone's throw from my father's new grave.

2

This was the "country" for a city child,
Arcadia, with grass, and trees
to chase around (*"Just keep
out of the way!"*)—giggly, racing wild

around the ancient headstones . . .
the Manhattan skyline, rising
like Oz on the horizon
beyond the flat bedroom borough.

The sun beating down on
plots and stones; on
live-forevers, and fresh yews,
and dry grass; on a slow

cortege climbing the narrow road;
on Chassidim, with curly earlocks and
black fedoras, selling prayers
along the sunbaked, treeless road.

3

A plot away, the separate graves of
my grandparents, rows apart,
separated in death. (Joe's parents,
who outlived him.)

FOREVER IN OUR HEARTS

My uncle Meyer (Joe's brother)
and aunt Chaika, nearby now; Tessie

Schmulowitz; Bessie Berkowitz;
the Polonetskys; the Lupitzkys; Sheine

Blume; Lizzie (died May 23, 1946,
age 69 years) and Aaron
(died November 22, 1931,
age 48 years) Loss;

Seltzer; Tobias; Lipschitz . . . Sanders?
Wilson? (names that don't sound like
family—maybe the family plots
a family "friend" sold privately).

"Put a stone on your uncle's grave."

My small white stone on his dark stone.
And stones for my grandparents,
separate in death. And, now,
a fresh stone on my father's fresh stone.

4

A stone's throw from my uncle's grave,
behind stone gates, carved with lions
and lyres, the comic and tragic masks of

THE YIDDISH THEATRICAL ALLIANCE

—my family rubbing elbows
with celebrities
(men on the left, women
on the right):

SKULNIK
Menasha

("gnomish" star
of my first Broadway show!)

May 15, 1890
June 4, 1970

Dear Husband

(the right side of the stone
still blank)

Ida Kaminska
Melman
1899–1980

Mother—Grandmother
Great-Grandmother

Bertha
Kalish
Spachner

May 17, 1874
April 28, 1939

(masks)

*To wake the soul by
tender strokes of art*

To raise the genius and
to mend the heart
To make mankind in
conscious virtue bold
Live o'er each scene and
be what they behold
For this the Tragic Muse
first trod the stage

(two masks: one smiling)

Maurice Schwartz
Founder, Director, Actor
of the
Yiddish Art Theatre

Pioneer	*of the*
&	*Yidish*
Founder	*Theatre*
	in America

(written on
pages of stone)

Bores
THOMASHEFSKY

Died
July 9, 1939
Age 73 years

Gone but not
forgotten

<pre>
M   F   M   A   X
    A   R
        X   I
                                 E
            H   D
                E   L
                    N   A
                        I   N
                            G   D
                                                 E
                                                     R

                                        S
                                    S
                                O
                        R
                    G

        E
      B
A
</pre>

(Headliners! Their names carved
diagonally: each headstone
a calling card, a billboard.
. . . *Where is the audience?*)

Dedicated to our
beloved father
Cesar
Greenberg
Died Dec. 27, 1932
Grandfather of the
Jewish stage
Playwriter, director,
and actor, covering
a period of 57 years

In memory of
our beloved
Joseph

Music   *Lyrics*
Joseph I. Tanzman
Playwright   *Comedian*

Born October 16, 1888
Departed
Apr. 4, 1931

Loving and kind
in all his ways
Upright and just,
To the end of his days
Sincere and true,
In his heart and mind
Beautiful memories,
He left behind

Joseph Lateiner
1853
1935
Yiddish Playwright

Yitzchok
Perlov
Writer   Journalist
and Poet

VEN ICH ZOL DICH FARLIREN

Max Kletter

("If I Should Lose You" . . .)

May 1, 1900
April 7, 1952

Cherished husband
beloved brother

(a photo under broken glass—suave, with
violin; and a bronze plaque)

> *My love,*
> *To our sorrow, God lent you to us for too short a time; yet,*
> *he let us keep forever: your heart—in your music; your*
> *warmth and zest—in your singing; your laughter—ringing*
> *in our ears; your love and devotion—implanted in our lives.*
> *Dearest, we lost the years we might have had, but we had*
> *the years we might have lost; so few, but so happy.*

You were a man to be proud of, my wonderful husband,
and the memory of you is a joy forever.

Louis Weiss
Beloved Father
Grandfather
Great-Grandfather
A man of wit and talent
admired by all

Saul Wallerstein
A pioneer in Yiddish theatre
Answered his last curtain call
March 13, 1933

Deeply mourned
by his wife, son, relatives
and friends.

Joseph Buloff. Goldie Goldman. Folksinger Lola Folman.
Leon Katz (his photo missing: IN OUR HEARTS
HE LIVES FOREVER). Pinchus Lawanda. David Licht. John
Saxon (real name: Yasha Kreitzberg). Benjamin Witaskin . . .

And one monument
without names—

Dedicated to the eternal
memory of the members
of the European Yiddish
theatrical profession

who were murdered by the
Nazis and other tyrants

Wives and husbands . . . cherished, dear;
devoted brothers, sisters; beloved
parents, and grandparents, and children:

　　FOREVER IN OUR HEARTS

—treading the boards, wearing their
masks:
　　　their names, their memorials, their

billing . . .

　　　　　GONE
　　　BUT NOT FORGOTTEN

　　　　DEEPLY MOURNED

Stone of memory.

　　　　5
On my father's fresh stone, I leave a stone.